P9-CBC-620

bold colors

sarah lynch

METRO BOOKS
NEW YORK

WELDON OWEN GROUP
Chief Executive Officer **John Owen**
Chief Financial Officer **Simon Fraser**

WELDON OWEN INC.
Chief Executive Officer and President **Terry Newell**
Senior VP, International Sales **Stuart Laurence**
VP, Sales and Marketing **Amy Kaneko**

VP, Creative Director **Gaye Allen**
Senior Art Director **Emma Boys**
Designers **Anna Giladi** and **Diana Heom**

VP, Publisher **Roger Shaw**
Executive Editor **Elizabeth Dougherty**
Managing Editor **Karen Templer**
Project Editor **Veronica Peterson**
Editorial Assistant **Sarah Gurman**

Production Director **Chris Hemesath**
Production Manager **Michelle Duggan**
Color Manager **Teri Bell**

A WELDON OWEN PRODUCTION
Copyright © 2008 Weldon Owen Inc.

Metro Books
122 Fifth Avenue
New York, NY 10011

ISBN-13: 978-1-4351-0757-1
ISBN-10: 1-4351-0757-8

Printed in China

10 9 8 7 6 5 4 3 2 1

5/2010 Barnes : Noble

contents

the power of color 8

blues 10

oranges 30

purples 44

yellows 62

reds 80

greens 100

pinks 116

blacks 128

the power of color

Many people proclaim how much they "love color," and what they likely mean is that they're not afraid to use lots of color in their lives. For others, color can seem daunting, whether for whole walls or a few throw pillows. There's no shame in being intimidated by bold colors—a trip to the paint store, with hundreds of colors in minutely varying shades, can overwhelm even a secure color fan.

When you're looking for a new palette or just one bold hue to perk up a space, it's a good idea to consult a color wheel, like the one to the right. Notice that the colors on the right half of the wheel, featuring yellows, oranges, and reds, have warm undertones. The left half—with its purples, blues, and greens—consists of colors that are cool. Use these underlying "temperatures" to your advantage when decorating. If you're looking for a refreshing space, choose a cool color. If you want a glowing room, select a warm hue.

Also consider the tried-and-true methods that designers use to arrive at successful color combinations. Colors that are neighbors on the wheel—such as greens, yellows, and oranges—automatically look at home as a group. Complementary colors are hues that sit directly across from each other on the wheel, such as blue and

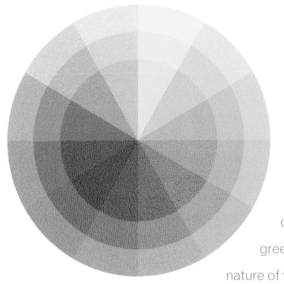

tool of the trade

Take the guesswork out of
choosing a palette by using
a color wheel, which maps
the relationships between
colors. As the pros know,
those are the key to mixing
colors successfully.

orange, or red and
green. Complements, by
nature of their contrast, make
each other appear more intense when paired. For that reason, a
color is often used with a lighter or darker shade of its complement.

Lastly, don't forget about the impact of black. Technically the
absence of color, black absorbs all hues in the spectrum and reflects
none of them. It is the perfect backdrop for an eye-catching piece
of furniture, it pairs beautifully with every color, and it instantly adds
drama and sophistication to any space.

This book is filled with inspirations, ideas, and tips for using colors
boldly, in all types of environments. If finding your perfect palette
seems a challenge, relax and enjoy the process. Once you've found
the right combination, the result will reward the effort.

blues

Cobalt, cornflower, royal blue, turquoise—if blue is your favorite color, you're far from alone. It's an easy color to love, and easily the most popular color in the rainbow. In a dining room or bedroom—and whatever the shade—blue will surely never go out of style.

using blue

Cool and calming, blue is a tried-and-true classic. It's a soothing shade that can be used to create a tranquil oasis, open up a room, or give your office a crisp look.

starry night

The relaxing nature of blue makes it a suitable choice for a bedroom. Many strong colors feel too vibrant for sleeping, but even the brightest cobalt or peacock blue can be simultaneously powerful and soothing.

cooling effects

Evocative of oceans and lakes, blue is also a fitting choice for a bath. Take care to select a shade that's not too pale, or the space might seem chilly. Wood elements will warm it up and balance out any white porcelain.

far and away

Blue is a receding color, meaning it looks farther away than it is. Painting the walls blue is a quick way to make a small space feel larger. Light blue ceilings suggest the sky and can also help make a room feel taller.

true colors

A blue room lit with harsh blue-white lights or green fluorescents can feel a bit like an institutional space. Warm up your blues by using incandescent bulbs in fixtures or by lighting candles to balance out the electric lights.

endless options

Blue looks terrific with essentially every color in the rainbow—think of the versatility of a pair of blue jeans. Anything you'd pair denim with, from deepest red to golden yellow to pure green, will look just as good in your rooms.

loyal blue

Have you ever wondered why politicians wear navy blue suits? Deep blue is associated with honesty and loyalty, which makes it an excellent choice for a home office or for any space where you'll be hosting potential clients.

stay awhile In a dining area, selecting welcoming shades of blue will encourage guests to pull up a chair, make themselves comfortable, and stay beyond dessert.

arth and sea

ocolate brown and
ades of turquoise
e an increasingly
pular combination.
x like textures, such
a velvet couch and
vety walls (left), or
milar patterns (right).

the perfect pair As seen in traditional delftware (above), rich blue is timeless when paired with crisp white. A glossy white ceiling counters this blue's duskiness.

viva aqua Covering surfaces with vibrant blue tiles—whether in a kitchen or a bathroom—is a bold way to bring the shimmering quality of the sea to an indoor spot.

great lengths

A lapis storage wall running
the length of this classical
hallway makes a dramatic
architectural statement.

wood accents add warmth to an expanse of bold color

Stainless steel plays up the coolness of navy blue, while a teak stool and box shelving, along with woven rattan bins, are earthy complements. Paler blue jars provide spots of accent color. White towels pop against this serene, spa-like backdrop.

mix and match

Botanical prints feel modern
when mixed with clean-lined
furnishings. Choose fabrics
or wallpapers in bright colors
to inject some personality into
a small space. Pair them with
softer tones for balance.

look on the upside The brilliant blue ceiling of this rustic room draws the eye upward. The rug, chairs, artwork, and other accent pieces echo the ceiling's hue.

oranges

A spot of orange is instantly energizing—just think about the feeling a fiery sunset or a ripe mango can evoke. If you want to breathe a little life into any room of the house that's feeling a bit drab, you can't go wrong with accent pieces—or full walls—in this vibrant hue.

using orange

Orange is energetic but can also come across as candy-colored. To counter that effect, use nuanced shades, pair them with softer colors, and keep it classic.

lasting effects

Orange has a tendency to cycle in and out of fashion. Skirt the trends by selecting shades that are somewhat more complex, such as coral, tangerine, or terra-cotta, and you're likely to enjoy them for a longer period.

the peach pit

It's a common mistake to try to "tone down" a bright color by adding white to the paint, which tends to result in timid pastels. In the case of orange, you'll wind up with peach. So pick a shade and stick with it.

good sport

For a powerful palette, pair orange with blue, which is its complement. To avoid the look of a sports team's clubhouse, consider variations on both colors: tangerine with periwinkle or deep persimmon with navy.

what a bargain

In advertising color theory, orange signals an inexpensive option: think fast-food chains and rental-car companies. Anything that is cheap plastic or at all poorly made could seem even chintzier in orange.

trial size

Orange can be a big commitment. Try using the color in a small space such as a powder room, or on a focal wall rather than over an entire room. Once you're accustomed to it, it's easy enough to start piling it on.

extra spicy

In a kitchen or dining room, true orange can feel a bit saccharine. A better background for meals are spicier shades, such as paprika, cumin, or saffron, which will enhance a meal rather than overwhelm it.

traveler's retreat Not for the shy and retiring, this bedroom gets its global flair from orange walls and tasseled silk lanterns, paired with a steamer trunk and globe.

all things equal

Bold accessories—a papaya
mohair throw and pillows,
turquoise goblets—look
sharp against a zebra print.

framing nature Taking color cues from autumn leaves and dried botanicals, this well-appointed outdoor living room feels as warm and welcoming as a campfire.

astern spice

erived from the
armest part of the
olor wheel, orange,
nk, and red create a
ensual setting. Sheer
anels delineate a
eeping space and
Id style to storage.

orange pop Feature just one orange element—a long, streamlined sofa or lacquered table—against a white background to add instant playfulness to a room.

purples

Depending on a purple's balance of red and blue, it can appear warm or cool. Many people associate purple with royalty, but it's also linked to creativity. Use bright purple to inspire and motivate. Consider soft lavender when you want a wonderfully tranquil effect.

using purple

You don't have to be a king or queen to surround yourself with this royal hue. Use it to add richness to a room, or to give candlelight some added drama.

go for baroque

Though subject to trends in most arenas, interior designers have used the complementary pairing of regal purple and metallic gold since Renaissance times. Go for a Baroque look by employing this duo in your home.

tranquility now

Heralded as a color with restorative properties, purple is the perfect hue to use in a luxury spa bath or a dressing room. Add towels and other linens in a cooler tint (or tints) of lavender to create a calm, contemplative mood.

wine notes

Warm purples look great by candlelight. Select a powerful shade of plum, eggplant, or cabernet for a dining room, living room, or bedroom—or anywhere there will be candles adding to an evening's festivities.

return of deco

For a daring yet classic palette, look to the colors of the Art Deco period. Aubergine, cranberry, teal, and gold have come back onto the runways, one after another, and the home design arena is sure to follow suit.

last not least

Violet, which lands at the very end of the color spectrum, is a hard color to categorize. With a bit more blue to it, violet creates an ethereal backdrop in any low-lit space, where it can't be easily identified.

purple reign

Purple's renewed and growing popularity has it popping up in unlikely spots—from kitchen appliances to bathroom fixtures and fabrics, to name just a few. As a result, purple now seems at home in any room.

friendly neighbors With combinations of magenta, purple, and indigo, these bedrooms demonstrate the innate harmony of hues adjacent on the color wheel.

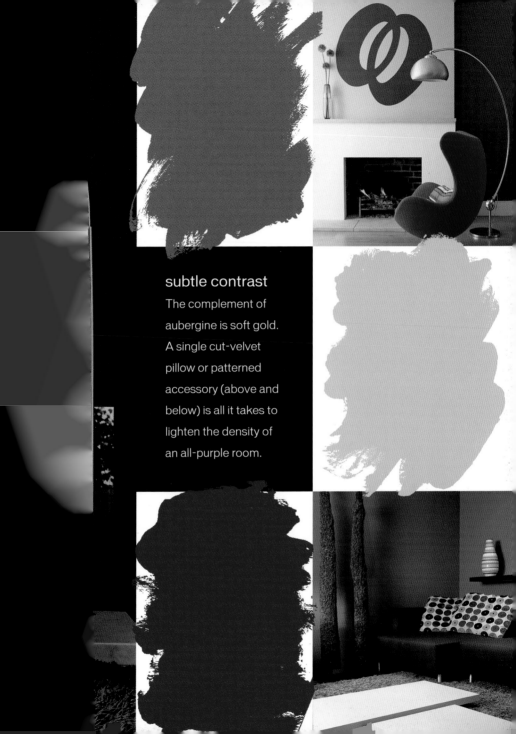

subtle contrast

The complement of
aubergine is soft gold.
A single cut-velvet
pillow or patterned
accessory (above and
below) is all it takes to
lighten the density of
an all-purple room.

seat of power Unexpected purple embellishments, such as the fringed silk cushions on these midcentury chairs, are an elegant touch in a neutral space.

the antineutral Red-purple looks even more vibrant behind cool stainless steel and warm wood. In a mix of patterns, it's equally at home in an all-white setting.

soft shading

Multiple tints of a hue
have natural harmony,
as seen in this dining
room. Earthy elements
balance out such bold
strokes as lilac lights
and modern chairs
recovered in lavender.

graphic designs

Saturated red and violet are an energetic pairing. Choose neutral colors and natural materials to tone down the vibrancy, or go all the way with modern chairs, oversize prints, and plastic accents.

exploring space Used broadly, dark plum almost magically recedes into the background, making pure white objects and interesting textures look more vivid.

yellows

Shades of yellow convey warmth and optimism, as they mimic the vital nature of sunshine. That's why yellow is so often described as "cheerful." Capitalize on the color's positive effects by sprinkling it generously throughout the house, or go all out in a single room.

using yellow

The only color whose brightness increases as it gets more saturated, yellow is fun to experiment with. Use it for dramatic effects or to add a hint of gentle cheer.

abandon caution

Roadside caution signs are in bright yellow and contrasting black so that they'll be spotted easily. Employ this eye-catching strategy and combine the two in any room that you want to ensure will never be overlooked.

here comes the sun

A sunny yellow bedroom can brighten the mood of a dreary day, but pick a shade that isn't overly saturated: bright yellow may feel overwhelming on a sunny morning and could make it hard to wind down at night.

neutral whites

Warm yellows look great in combination with pure white in a kitchen. White can also help neutralize the yellow, which was shown in at least one study to promote more arguments than any other color when used on walls.

bright lights

Yellow, like other warm colors, will turn greenish under fluorescent lighting and look peachy under rosy incandescents. To get the truest rendering of your selected shade of yellow, you'll want to opt for full-spectrum lighting.

primary school

Yellow looks great as part of a citrusy palette (that is, with orange and lime) or as an accent for brown or gray. The trio of primary colors—yellow, red, and blue—will evoke a kids' playroom, whether or not that's your aim.

power of purple

Yellow's complement is purple, so if a canary yellow chair isn't as wild as you'd expected, toss in an eggplant pillow. From pale lavender to deep plum, accents of purple will up the intensity of any shade of yellow.

sunny disposition This ultra-contemporary, stainless-steel kitchen would feel plainly industrial without its quirky yellow walls and ceiling, and its accents of red.

a welcome note

Sunflower yellow walls make a clear statement in an entryway: the vibe of this house is bright and breezy.

fresh picked Lemon yellow looks especially harmonious with lime green. Use the two in matched saturation and equal amounts to make the most of the pairing.

sun salutation

Allover yellow mosaic tiles
blur the boundaries of this
small bath and set off sleek
fixtures in pristine porcelain.

time and again Golden yellow is a surprisingly timeless hue. Notice how this antique table and vintage shawl-style tablecloth add vibrancy to these rooms.

bend the rules

The boldest statements are often the result of flouting tradition. Here the duo of red and yellow—considered a faux pas by many—is used unapologetically. The black wall intensifies the palette.

easy choice Yellow is bold without being overbearing. When incorporating another primary, such as blue, use softened shades, to avoid a playhouse look.

reds

You can't go wrong with red—it's practically the neutral of the bold color palette. Suitable for even the most traditional styles, red declares confidence and sophistication. A bold sweep of crimson on any surface is the fastest way to make a statement.

using red

Never underestimate the power of red. As long as you don't let it overpower you or your rooms, it's a great choice for perking up traditional and modern decors.

hot stuff

An advancing color—one that reaches the human eye faster than other colors—red can make walls feel closer and the room smaller. It's also a hot color, so choose a space big enough and cool enough to handle it.

season's greetings

When using red with its complement, green, it's better not to use both at their full saturation—you'll wind up with a room that begs a Christmas tree. To give red the starring role, use a muted gray-green such as sage or moss.

exotic locale

Pairing red with either hot pink or orange has long been a no-no. But a palette of all three—red, pink, and orange—has recently come into vogue. Set against warm wood tones, it evokes tropical getaways or the Far East.

perfect match

Anything but the truest red will have either a little bit of orange or purple in it. Placed side by side, these minor variations will be amplified. So choose a shade of red you like and keep a swatch handy for matching purposes.

rosy glow

All bright colors will cast a reflection on anything near them—in red's case, it's pink. So keep that in mind when planning a red-painted room: as soon as you turn on the lights, everything will take on a rosy appearance.

modern red

Accents of red give life to a modern, minimalist space. Red goes well with almost any building material—from steel to wood to concrete—yet holds its own in the presence of even the boldest architecture.

common thread

An intense color such as fire-engine red can tie differing spaces together, as seen with the wall, stools, throw, and pillows in this lofty, mixed-use room.

Menú del día

Gambas con jamon
Ensalada de Perist
y
Plan

Vinos - de Candela

repeat appearance Take advantage of red's appetite-inducing properties by using it in a dining room or kitchen. Rows of chairs or glasses multiply the impact.

sleep patterns

Red and white is an arresting combination. Make the classic look your own by mixing patterns, such as toile, wide stripes, gingham, and assorted plaids.

red-handed Flowers, paintings, and prints in your favorite crimson hue can enliven an otherwise neutral room (left), or add impact to an already bold space.

everyday red

If you love red but
want a warmer look,
choose a softer shade
for walls—such as
brick red or deep
cinnabar—combine it
with wood, and pick
true-red accessories

center of attention Red is so eye-catching that any note will always stand out. Paired with avocado in a mainly black-and-white room, this red chair is the star.

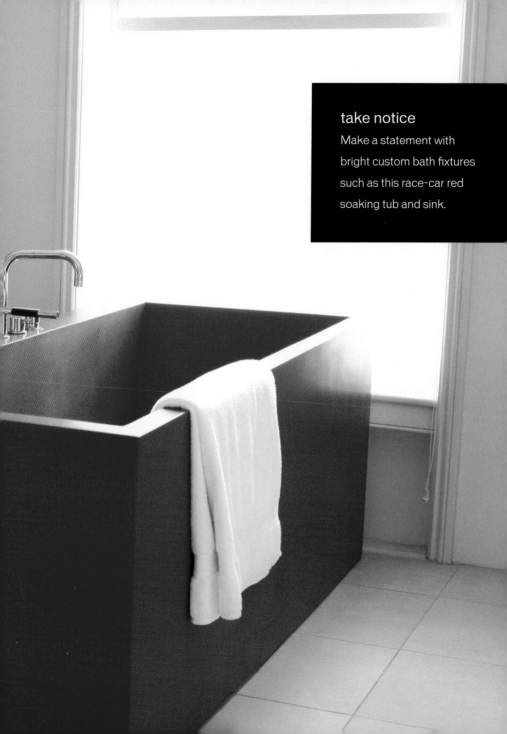

take notice

Make a statement with bright custom bath fixtures such as this race-car red soaking tub and sink.

seeing red Shallow red lacquer cabinets seem to pop right out of their wood and glass surround, as does a red car in a Cuban street-scene photograph.

greens

From shocking chartreuse to the earthiest olive, green is accessible and complex at the same time. As it has more variations visible to the human eye than any other color, picking just the right shade of green can be a challenge—but then again, why limit yourself to one?

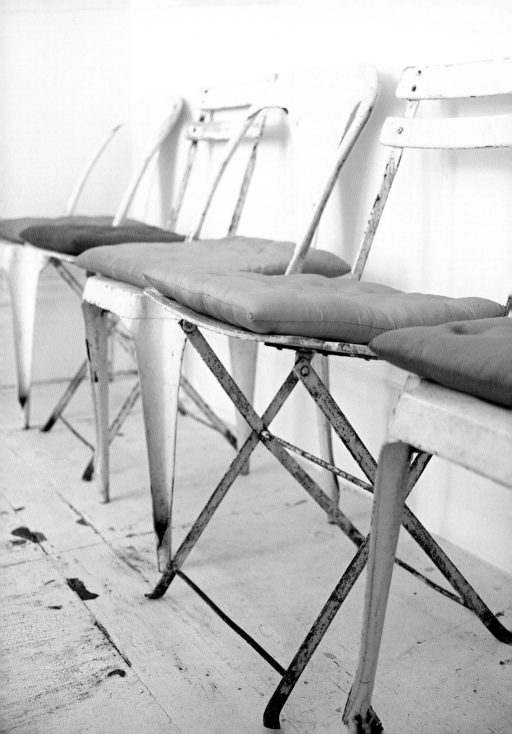

using green

The friendly spirit of green makes it ideal for shared spaces. Whether you're evoking nature or adding get-up-and-go accents, it's good to be green.

swatch watch

The spectrum of greens runs from teal at the blue end to chartreuse at the yellow end, which can make it tricky to shop for things that match. Keep a swatch with you, because your "pistachio" may be another person's "lime."

natural selections

When using green and red together, picture a bouquet of cut flowers. Red tulips in a bunch will be roughly one-quarter red and the rest green. Following this ratio can lend your scheme the right amount of punch.

accessibly bold

Unlike most other colors, where bold often means bright, green offers a wealth of approachable shades. If you want to make a bold statement but are intimidated by the likes of coral and violet, try a wall of vivid olive.

great outdoors

Use green anywhere you want the clean feeling of the outdoors. A tonal palette of various shades of green—keep it to no more than five—can make even a room with limited windows feel like an indoor-outdoor space.

green light

Green means go, so use it anywhere you need a call to action, such as in a home office or laundry room. To maximize the effect, choose apple, lime, or any other bright shade that strikes you as inspiring and motivating.

in good health

Grassy green has gained a new connotation in recent years, through its use in packaging and ad campaigns to indicate healthy or earth-friendly choices. It's a statement that will translate to any room you apply it to.

balancing act Jade green is a good candidate for a complementary color scheme. Here, it's used lavishly enough to balance out even the boldest of reds.

private rain forest

Nature's influence is evident in this inviting bathroom, where the leafy green tiled shower is complemented by terra-cotta floor tiles. Sand-colored Venetian plaster on the walls adds to the room's earthiness.

floral notes A tip from the flower market: chocolate cosmos suggest a bright and unexpected color combination—lime green with gold and deepest purple.

attention grabber Use a color like kelly green to highlight features that might go unnoticed, such as shelves backed by chartreuse (above) or interior shutters.

GILBERT & GEORGE
DE KOONING

RUSSISCHE AVANTGARDE - KUNST
DUMONT   DIE SAMMLUNG GEORGE COSTAKIS

ll candy

ou love color and
't pick just one,
ect a few favorites
use them broadly
heighboring walls.
nctuate them with
phic artwork in
ally vibrant hues.

along the grain

Typical of the California Arts
and Crafts style is this mix of
gray-green and warm woods.
Originally inspired by a forest
of redwoods, it's a look that's
right at home with indoor
greenery and outdoor views.

pinks

It takes a courageous soul to love hot pink, and an even more courageous one to decorate with it. Sure, it's traditionally associated with girliness—sugar and spice and everything nice—but if you're in touch with your playful side, and ready to show it off, pink is for you.

using pink

Everyone looks good in pink—though few realize it—so don't let the doubters faze you. Since pink can work in just about any room, you'll be sitting pretty in no time.

palatable pink

Be careful to choose the right pink for the function of a space. In a dining area, bubble-gum pink may seem unappealing. Try matching the shade of something you might serve—a chilled borscht or a raspberry sorbet.

nurturing nature

In a bedroom, pinks are especially flattering. When decorating a room for a child, go all out with a mix of pink and purple. To create a more elegant space for grown-ups, pair magenta with gray, or soft pink with an earthy green.

one-hit wonder

Sometimes a single item in hot pink—a vibrant velvet chair or a mohair throw—in an otherwise neutral space is enough to increase the color quotient. Even in small doses, pink can make a powerful statement.

opposites attract

Lime green sits directly across from pink on the color wheel, and, unlike so many complementary combinations, they make a popular duo. Use both hues at full saturation to conjure up springtime or classic preppy flair.

petal soft

Flowery pink is an ideal choice for a bathroom, where it's charming while also seeming to be softly scented. Alternatively, a warmer reddish pink can be soothing when you step out of the shower on a cold winter's morning.

femme fatale

For those who fear the connotations of "pink," take refuge in the names. Steer clear of anything described as "rose" or "petal," and opt for more complex and elegant choices, such as "coral," "salmon," and "zinnia."

back in time

Cotton-candy pink is a color that almost unavoidably suggests 1950s nostalgia. Pairing it with cherry-red accents or modern acrylic furnishings can give that nod to the past a playful twist.

pop art As complements, green and pink can be combined in a variety of ways. Here, the colors of cherry blossoms and jade support an Asian-inspired theme.

new traditions

Prove that even the most traditional homes can have a sense of humor by combining daring shades of hot pink, magenta, and purple in an otherwise classic bathroom.

exercising control To keep fuchsia from feeling too over-the-top, use it in controlled doses–a pattern or piece of art–in an otherwise black-and-white space.

blacks

Beige, sage, and chocolate have ruled the design world for so long that black and gray can seem like daring choices. Conventional wisdom says every room needs something black, but rooms that fully embrace this anticolor might just be the boldest of them all.

using black

Many people who aren't timid about wearing black shy away from decorating with it. Used wisely, shades of black can add depth and drama to your decor.

to the touch

Working with muted colors provides the perfect opportunity to go bold with texture and pattern. If embossed wall finishes, embroidered fabric, or faux fur seems too loud for you, consider them in a soft black.

shining star

White reflects light, while black absorbs it. You can counter this darkening effect by incorporating shiny surfaces—such as high-gloss paint, leather, or laminate—into a room to keep the space from feeling gloomy.

stark contrast

Freshen up black or gray with pure white. (Pure white can be difficult to find, as most whites have undertones of either blue or yellow.) For a quieter but still stylish contrast, try pairing charcoal gray with the palest ivory.

depth of character

To the human eye, dark gray seems to have more depth to it than other colors. Capitalize on that character trait in a small room by painting walls gray—or a color with lots of gray in it—to make the space feel larger.

test patch

Blacks and grays, each a blend of many colors, may appear to be dark shades of other colors in differing light. When painting walls, paint a test square and observe it at various times of day, and under different lighting.

traditional twist

Ditching its association with the industrial-chic furnishings of the 1980s, black is now being used by cutting-edge designers to update the look of classic pieces, such as a French Country armchair or a Louis XVI chest.

studied minimalism

In a predominantly white room with lofty ceilings, French doors, and ample windows, black acts as a point of reference. The giant tufted ottoman, black furniture legs, and ebonized wood floors work in tandem to ground the space. The gilt accents, spare sofa, and oversize mirror keep the room light and bright.

high contrast Enhance the impact of a graphic black-and-white pattern with a spot of contrast—a pink blanket or an earthenware vase and branches of greenery.

set a scene

Nothing could show off the
curvaceousness of these
vintage-inspired porcelain
fixtures quite like black.

rethinking gray

The truest neutral, medium gray gracefully balances a bright shade like goldenrod. The gray's softness takes the edge off the pulsating yellow while highlighting it at the same time.

stone age

The same variegated
tile covers every inch
of this minimalist bath,
maximizing the subtle
variations of black,
gray, and silver found
in a slab of stone.

the perfect foil

A purely black-and-white
setting—right down to the
pottery—heightens the colors
and textures of everything that
enters the scene: blue-gray
metal chairs, orange fruit, pink
flowers—even a straw bag.

photo credits:

front **cover** Taverne Agency/Alexander van Berge/production Ulrika Lundgren; **1** Getty Images/Michael Grimm; **2** Photozest/Inside/M Roobaert; **4-5** Red Cover/Marc Broussard/designer Yves Taralon; **6-7** Camera Press London/Côté Sud/Bernard Touillon; **11** Getty Images/Amy Neunsinger; **12** Arcaid/Belle/Simon Kenny; **14** IPC Syndication/*Living Etc.*/ Jake Curtis; **15** Taverne Agency/Alexander van Berge/production Ulrika Lundgren; **16** Jim Franco; **19** IPC Syndication/*Homes & Gardens*/Tom Leighton; **20** Camera Press London/*Marie Claire Maison*/Vincent Leroux; **21** Photozest/Inside/H & L/S Inggs; **22-23** Lluis Casals; **26** Red Cover/ Grey Crawford; **27** Mainstream Images/Ray Main; **31** Taverne Agency/Nathalie Krag/Tami Christiansen; **43** Photozest/C Fiorentini; **45** IPC Syndication/*Amateur Gardening*; **48** Getty Images/ Michael Grimm; **49** Red Cover/Ed Reeves; **50, 51 (top)** Alamy/Key Collections/real; **51 (bottom)** Alamy/Lourens Smak; **54** Camera Press London/*Marie Claire Maison*/Vincent Leroux; **56** Getty Images; **58** IPC Syndication/*Living Etc.*/Jake Curtis; **61** IPC Syndication/*Living Etc.*/David Hiscock; **63** Red Cover/Di Lewis; **64** Fab-pics/E Pons; **72-73** Arcaid/Grzywinski Pons Architects; **76-77** IPC Syndication/*Living Etc.*/Chris Everard; **79** IPC Syndication/*Living Etc.*/Paul Massey; **81** Narratives/Jan Baldwin; **86** Joseph De Leo; **87** Photozest/Inside/A Barahle; **90** Andreas von Einsiedel/interior design Esther Fitzgerald; **91** Fab-pics; **94-95** Andreas von Einsiedel/interior design Gareth Devonald Smith; **96-97** Red Cover/Verity Welstead; **98** Camera Press, London/Lisa Linder; **101** IPC Syndication/*Living Etc.*/Tom Leighton; **104** Camera Press, London/*Marie Claire Maison*/Catherine Ardouin/Mia-Linh; **105** IPC Syndication/*Country Homes & Interiors*/Gloria Nicol; **108** Getty Images/Michael Grimm; **110** Red Cover/Robin Matthews; **111** Mainstream Images/Ray Main; **117** Robert Trachtenberg/painting Alison Van Pelt; **120** Mark Lund; **122-123** IPC Syndication/ *Marie Claire*/Tom Leighton; **126** IPC Syndication/*Living Etc.*/Craig Knowles; **127** Andreas von Einsiedel/architect Sproson Barrable/design Elizabeth Brooks/painting Sara Rossberg; **129** Mainstream Images/Ray Main; **130** Narratives/Jan Baldwin/decorator Cecile & Boyd's/Singita Sweni Lodge, South Africa; **133** Andreas von Einsiedel/design John Minshaw; **136-137** Camera Press, London/*Marie Claire Maison*/Laurent Teisseire; **138** Mainstream Images/Ray Main; **140, 141 (top)** Taverne Agency/Nathalie Krag/Tami Christiansen; **back cover (right)** Jim Franco; **back cover (left)** IPC Syndication/*Country Homes & Interiors*/Gloria Nicol.

57 (top), 106 (right), 141 (bottom) Emma Boys; **52-53, 55, 75, 78, 92, 135, 142-143** Hotze Eisma; **36-37, 60, 67, 118, 121** Lisa Romerein; **17, 28-29** (painting Margarett Sargent), **32, 66, 68-69, 112-113** Eric Roth.

All other photography © Weldon Owen Inc./Pottery Barn: **24-25, 106 (left), 107, 124, 125 (top)** Hotze Eisma; **71** Mark Lund; **102** Stefano Massei; **39, 57 (bottom), 74, 93, 109, 115, 125 (bottom)** David Matheson; **34-35, 40-41, 59, 82, 88-89, 134** Prue Ruscoe; **18, 38, 42, 46, 70, 84-85, 99, 114, 132 (left), 139 (top and bottom)** Alan Williams.

Special thanks to photography researchers Nadine Bazar and Sarah Airey.